For

HOLIDAY
Toasts & Graces

Edited by Barbara Kohn

Design by Deborah Michel

Illustrations by Grace De Vito

PETER PAUPER PRESS, INC.
WHITE PLAINS · NEW YORK

Dedicated with a loving
toast to Bob Welsh

Jacket background illustration by Grace De Vito
Jacket oval inset illustration by Linda DeVito Soltis

Contents

Introduction to Holiday Toasts

oasting was practiced by the ancient Greeks and continued by the Romans. The latter, known for their infamous bacchanals, considered toasting one another's health so important that the Senate decreed that all must drink to

Augustus Caesar at every meal. It was the British, however, who, in the 17th Century, named the custom of drinking to one another a "toast." To add flavor or nourishment to the drink, implying that the honoree had a special flavor of his or her own, a piece of toast or crouton was dropped into the goblet.

*T*oday's toast may be convivial, sentimental, inspirational, poetic, eloquent, satiric, or witty. As an opener at state dinners and receptions, the toast is often an expression of hope for peace and improved relations.

*I*t may be short, such as Bogart's to Bergman in "Casablanca:" *Here's looking at you, kid,* or it may be as long as the beautiful and spiritual familiar Irish toast to life: *May the*

road rise up to meet you, may the wind be always at your back, the sun shine warm upon your face, the rain fall soft upon your fields, and until we meet again, may God hold you in the hollow of His hand.

*Y*ou will find in this collection of toasts something timely and appropriate for that special person or festive occasion. So lift your glass, whether it holds champagne or fruit juice, and celebrate!

Toasts from Around the World

A LA SALUTE; SALUTE; CIN CIN: ITALY

A SUA SAÚDE: PORTUGAL

A VOTRE SANTÉ; SANTÉ: FRANCE

CHEERS: ENGLAND

DOWN THE HATCH: UNITED STATES

EIS IGIAN: GREECE

FEE SIHETAK: EGYPT

IECHYD DA: WALES

JAIKIND; AANAND: INDIA

KAMPAI; BANZAI: JAPAN

KIPPIS; MALJANNE: FINLAND

KONG GANG UL WI HA YO: KOREA

L'CHAYIM: ISRAEL

NA ZDRAVI; NAZDAR: CZECHOSLOVAKIA

NA ZDOROVIA: RUSSIA

NA ZDROWIE; VIVAT: POLAND

NIEN NIEN NU E; KONG CHIEN; KONG CHIEN;

KAN BEI; YUM SEN: CHINA

9

OKOLE MALUINA: HAWAII

OP UW GEZONHEID: BELGIUM

PROOST; GELUCH: HOLLAND

PROSIT: GERMANY

SALUD: MEXICO, SPAIN

SAÚDE; VIVA: BRAZIL

SAWASDI: THAILAND

SEREFE: TURKEY

SKÅL: DENMARK, NORWAY, SWEDEN

Toasts
for
Special Occasions

May the saddest day of the future
Be no worse than the happiest
day of the past!

IRISH TOAST

11

*H*ere's to you, as good as you are,
And here's to me, as bad as I am;
But as good as you are, and as bad as I am,
I am as good as you are, as bad as I am.

OLD SCOTTISH TOAST

*M*ay your joys be as deep as the ocean and
your sorrows as light as the foam.

JACOB M. BRAUDE

*B*e at war with your voices, at peace with
your neighbors, and let every new year find you
a better man.

BENJAMIN FRANKLIN

$\mathscr{M}$ay all your troubles be little ones.

WEDDING TOAST

$\mathscr{T}$o temperance . . . in moderation.

LEM MOTLOW

$\mathscr{D}$rink! for you know not
whence you came, nor why:
Drink! for you know not why
you go, nor where.

RUBAIYAT OF OMAR KHAYYAM

13

*H*ere's to the maiden of bashful fifteen;
Here's to the widow of fifty;
Here's to the flaunting, extravagant queen,
And here's to the housewife that's thrifty.
  Let the toast pass—
  Drink to the lass;
I'll warrant she'll prove an excuse for the glass.

RICHARD B. SHERIDAN

*M*ay the Force be with you.

ALEC GUINNESS,
STAR WARS

14

$\mathcal{T}$o the old, long life and treasure;
To the young, all health and pleasure.

BEN JONSON

$\mathcal{H}$ere's mud in your eye!

FROM AMERICAN FRONTIER DAYS

$\mathcal{H}$ere's to the happy man: All the world loves a lover.

RALPH WALDO EMERSON

$\mathcal{D}$o not resist growing old—
Many are denied the privilege!

IRISH TOAST

15

*M*ay you live all the days of your life.

JONATHAN SWIFT

*M*ay you live as long as you want,
And want to as long as you live.

ANONYMOUS

*Y*ou're not as young as you used to be
But you're not as old as you're going to be
So watch it!

IRISH TOAST

$\mathcal{M}$ay the good Lord take a liking to you—but not too soon!

<small>IRISH TOAST</small>

$\mathcal{B}$read—to feed our friendship,
Salt—to keep it true,
Water—that's for welcome,
Wine—to drink to you!

<small>FRENCH TOAST</small>

$\mathcal{T}$he good die young—
Here's hoping you live to a ripe old age.

<small>ANONYMOUS</small>

*M*ay peace come to those who make love
And love come to those who make peace.

BARBARA KOHN

*A*llow me to raise a glass to the work that
has been done, the work that remains to be
done. And let us also toast the art of friendly
persuasion, the hope of peace with freedom, the
hope of holding out for a better way of settling
things.

PRESIDENT RONALD REAGAN,
TO MIKHAIL GORBACHEV, 1989

*H*ere's tae us; wha's like us?
Gey few, and they're a' deid.

OLD SCOTTISH TOAST

$\mathcal{W}$ho loves not women, wine, and song,
Remains a fool his whole life long.

JOHANN HEINRICH VOSS

$\mathcal{H}$ere's to us that are here, to you that are there, and the rest of us everywhere.

RUDYARD KIPLING

$\mathcal{T}$o peace and friendship among all people.

PRESIDENT JIMMY CARTER, *1979*

$\mathcal{M}$ay you be in Heaven half an hour before the Devil knows you are dead!

IRISH TOAST

$\mathcal{N}$ow let us sit and drink and
   make us merry,
And afterward we will his body
   bury.

GEOFFREY CHAUCER,
THE CANTERBURY TALES

$\mathcal{D}$rink to-day, and drown all sorrow;
You shall perhaps not do it to-morrow.

FLETCHER AND MASSINGER,
THE BLOODY BROTHER, C. 1616

$\mathcal{M}$ay our house always be too small to hold
all our friends.

MYRTLE REED

$\mathcal{L}$et the fruits of the earth not widen your girth.

Barbara Kohn

$\mathcal{I}$ wish you health,
I wish you wealth,
I wish you happiness galore,
I wish you heaven when you die,
What could I wish you more?

Irish Toast

$\mathcal{A}$s you slide down the
   bannister of life
May the splinters never face
   the wrong way!

Irish Toast

*M*ay there always be work for
your hands to do
May your purse always hold a
coin or two
May the sun always shine on
your windowpane
May a rainbow be certain to
follow each rain
May the hand of a friend
always be near you
May God fill your heart with
gladness—and cheer you!

IRISH TOAST

*M*ay your mornings be hopeful
Your afternoons be fruitful
And all your nights be tranquil.

BARBARA KOHN

May the luck of the Irish possess you
May the Devil fly off with your worries
May God bless you forever and ever!

IRISH TOAST

Drink to me only with thine eyes,
  And I will pledge with mine;
Or leave a kiss but in the cup,
  And I'll not look for wine.
The thirst that from the soul
doth rise
  Doth ask a drink divine;
But might I of Jove's nectar sup,
  I would not change for thine.

BEN JONSON

$\mathcal{W}$hen you ascend the hill of prosperity may you not meet a friend.

MARK TWAIN

$\mathcal{D}$rink not to my past, which is
  weak and indefensible,
Nor to my present, which is not
  above reproach;
But let us drink to our futures,
  which, thank God, are
  immaculate.

LEONE P. FORKNER

Toasts

for

Holidays

FOR THE NEW YEAR

*R*ing out the old, ring in the new,
Ring, happy bells, across the snow:
The year is going, let him go;
Ring out the false, ring in the true.

ALFRED, LORD TENNYSON,
IN MEMORIAM

*M*ay this year be the best you've ever had
And the worst of those to come.

LEE SHARPLESS

And surely ye'll be your pint stowpt,
   And surely I'll be mine,
And we'll tak' a cup o' kindness yet,
   For auld lang syne.
For auld lang syne, my dear,
   For auld lang syne,
We'll tak' a cup o' kindness yet,
   For auld lang syne.

ROBERT BURNS

May we live by the nguzo saba (seven reasons or principles). May the year's end meet us laughing and stronger. And at the end of next year, may more of us sit together. May we achieve a better life . . . May your Kwanzaa be happy.

A. P. PORTER

FOR VALENTINE'S DAY

To my Valentine:
I love you
Not only for what you are,
But what I am
When I am with you.

ROY CROFT

28

For St. Patrick's Day

*M*ay the Leprechauns be near
   you to spread luck along your way
And may all the Irish angels
   smile upon you on St. Pat's Day!

IRISH TOAST

For Mother's Day

*T*o Mom:

I love you less for what you did for me than for
what you taught me to do for myself.

BARBARA KOHN

FOR FATHER'S DAY

*M*ay we always be there for you as you have been there for us.

BARBARA KOHN

FOR INDEPENDENCE DAY

*M*y toast would be, may our country be always successful, but whether successful or otherwise, always right.

JOHN QUINCY ADAMS

For Labor Day

*E*very man should eat and drink, and enjoy
the good of all his labor, it is the gift of God.

ECCLESIASTES 3:13 (KJV)

For Thanksgiving

*T*o the harvest-time of year
  When Plenty pours her wine of cheer,
And even humble boards may spare
  To poorer poor a kindly share.

ANONYMOUS

31

FOR CHRISTMAS

God bless us every one! said Tiny Tim, the last of all.

CHARLES DICKENS,
A CHRISTMAS CAROL

Peace on earth, good will toward men.

FROM THE SONG *COME TO THE MANGER*

Christmas Day is come; let's all
     prepare for mirth
Which fills the heav'ns.

LUKE WADDING,
CHRISTMAS DAY IS COME

Introduction

to
Table Graces

 able graces are prayers of thanks to God offered at the beginning of a meal. A simple grace such as *Lord, we thank Thee for the food we are about to receive. Amen* is sufficient.

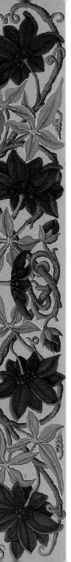

*H*owever, a grace can also be longer, more poetic or spiritual, and more thought-provoking. In any event, saying different graces at breakfast or dinner, at various holidays and times of year, or in response to a recent sermon or the news of the day enhances the spiritual and intellectual content of the experience.

*T*able graces bring a family together, keep us in touch with God and help us to remember our fellow men and women in need. Many people link hands as a physical symbol of the link between family and friends and between those at the table and all of God's children on earth.

*W*hatever words of praise we utter, God will hear our voices and understand our meaning. As an unknown poet once said:

*L*ord of the Universe, I am a simple man, an ignorant man. Oh, how I wish I had the words to fashion beautiful prayers to praise Thee! But alas, I cannot find these words. So listen to me, O God, as I recite the letters of the alphabet. You know what I think and how I feel. Take these letters of the alphabet and You form the words that express the yearning, the love for Thee that is in my heart.

*M*ore than a quarter of the graces in this book were compiled or composed years ago by Paul Simpson McElroy, a contemporary religious thinker. New graces, especially those with modern themes, were composed by Evelyn and Nick Beilenson. And the reader will find to his or her delight many familiar traditional graces, as well as adaptations of a number of well-known graces.

Graces
for Holidays
and Special
Occasions

NEW YEAR'S DAY

*A*s we gather around the festive board this beautiful New Year's Day, we thank Thee dear Lord for Thy goodness to us, and pray God the hungry everywhere may be fed. Be with us during this day, guide and keep us, we ask in His name. Amen.

ASH WEDNESDAY

O God, we think of the sins we have committed, and we repent and ask Thy forgiveness. We rely on Thy everlasting mercy. In the good food and drink that are placed before us, we look for Your strength to preserve us. Amen.

Palm Sunday

On this holy day we meditate on our Saviour, the Prince of Peace, whom You have sent into this world to redeem us from sin. Inspire us to accept Him as our Lord, and we say with gratitude—Amen.

Good Friday

Lord, we ask You to bless our food on this day which commemorates our crucified Lord. We are with Him as He carries His cross to Calvary Mount. May we accept Christ and this food with humility and with love. Amen.

PASSOVER

*B*lessed are You, God, Creator of the Universe, who brings forth from the earth the fruit of the vine. Blessed are You, God, Creator of the Universe, who sanctified our people by giving us commandments to fulfill, and who makes us joyful by giving us holidays for celebration. Tonight we celebrate the Festival of Pesach to remember a holy event in our history: our liberation from slavery in Egypt.

EASTER

*T*his day, O Christ, we celebrate Thy victory over death. Bring to us new life of body through this nourishment, and new life of soul by Thy presence with us now and help us to say with Thy servant of old: *Thanks be to God which giveth us the victory through Jesus Christ our Lord.* Amen.

*A*t this Easter sunrise, we are inspired by the tidings of eternal life through the risen Christ, Thy only son. With gratitude we ask blessing for this food now set before us, in Jesus' name. Amen.

MOTHER'S DAY

❧⚬❧⚬❧

*T*oday we give special thanks to our mothers, whether here on earth or departed, who have loved us and guided us from infancy to maturity. Amen.

MEMORIAL DAY

❧⚬❧⚬❧

*L*ord, we remember those brave Americans who gave their lives to protect our country's physical integrity and its ways of democracy and freedom. They died so that we could live in peace and tranquility. We give thanks that we can today come together at this table with abundant food, in harmony and in peace. Amen.

FATHER'S DAY

*O*n this special day we remember what is true all year long, that our fathers through love and pride have helped us to become responsible and loving human beings. We are the better because of our fathers' guiding examples. Amen.

INDEPENDENCE DAY

*W*e ask Thy blessing today upon this glorious Republic. Shield her from error, guard her from corruption, make of her a nation after Thine own heart. For the liberty whose birthday we celebrate today, we give Thee gracious thanks, especially for the liberty of serving Thee according as Thou dost give us wisdom. Vouchsafe Thy continued providence over us, and eventually may we be gathered at Thy right hand in glory. Amen.

LABOR DAY

*A*s we ask Thy blessing upon our home today, we ask too that Thou wilt graciously bless the homes of all those who live by the sweat of their brow. Give us the health to labor on, and grace to be proud of labor, remembering the example of our Lord, and His word of commendation that the laborer is worthy of his hire. Continue with us this day and evermore. Amen.

THANKSGIVING DAY

Once more we come, Lord, to this day of special thanksgiving. Our thoughts are turned backward, to the Pilgrims and Indians and also to this past year. The days have rolled into the seasons, the seasons into the year. Each day has been crowded with Thee. Each season has brought forth new proofs of Thy loving forethought. May we this day pledge Thee our gratitude anew. Amen.

CHRISTMAS MORNING

We thank Thee for the blessings received during the days that are gone, and ask Thy Divine blessing upon this food this Holy Christmas morning, for Jesus' sake. Amen.

CHRISTMAS EVENING

༄

*W*e thank Thee for this day's feast, instituted
by the Birth of Thy Holy Son. Bless us and
guide us through all time, we ask for Jesus' sake.
Amen.

NEW YEAR'S EVE

༄

*T*onight we celebrate that we have lived yet
another year wrapped in Thy warm embrace.
Throughout this past year, Thy love has
sustained us. We ask that, in the year to come,
Thou guide us along the straight and narrow
path to Thy love. Amen.

Table Graces

for

All Times

*Lord, help us to receive all good things
as from Thy hand,
and to use them to Thy praise.
Amen.*

$\mathcal{D}$ear Lord, who openest Thy hand and fillest the earth with good, and hast provided Thy children sufficient to satisfy all our needs; teach us to render back to Thee Thy due thanksgiving, not only in words, but also in the manner of our living. Amen.

$\mathcal{A}$s we join hands, let us come together, rich and poor, black and white, young and old, enjoying each other's uniqueness. Just as each season brings a new loveliness, so does each man and woman bring forth a special gift, making this world a more beautiful place to live in. Amen.

$\mathcal{L}$ord, we are grateful for this family, which hand in hand forms one unbroken circle. Help us to do Thy will, as caring individuals and as a loving family. Amen.

*L*ord, we are the children of the age of technology. We rush through our busy days often mindless of what we eat and what we drink. In the name of expediency we lose sight of nature's wonderful gifts. Sometimes we do not come to the table as a family to enjoy the harvest of Your creation. Lord, help us to be mindful of Your gifts. Amen.

*F*or bright lights and warm fires,
    We thank Thee, O God;
For good food and the clothes we wear,
    We thank Thee, O God;
For the love and care of mother and father,
    We thank Thee, O God;
For friends who come to be our guests,
    We thank Thee, O God;
For all things You have given us to enjoy,
    We thank Thee, O God;
For true happiness which comes when we share,
    We thank Thee, O God.

48

$\mathcal{L}$ord, help us to remember when it is easy to forget those less fortunate than ourselves. While we sit at this table surrounded by family and friends, others are lost and alone. While we share bread, others go hungry. While we are sheltered from the cold, others are homeless. Lord, help us to remember the poor and needy, and be thankful. Amen.

$\mathcal{A}$s teenagers we come before Thee and give thanks for the strength and awareness that come each day as we bridge the difficult journey from childhood to adulthood. God sustains us in school and shares our joy. As our minds and bodies grow may we be ever mindful of the physical and spiritual nourishment which God's presence provides. Amen.

$\mathcal{L}$ord, we are the stewards of Your beneficence to our earth. Help us to act so that the food which You set before us today and in the future may be free from chemical pollutants and radioactive contamination. Help us to make technology bend to our deepest needs. Help us, O Lord, to make our world a better place. Amen.

$\mathcal{S}$o much of the world goes to bed hungry every night, but we are blessed with abundance. The bellies of Third World children swell through malnutrition, but we have more food than we need. We wonder what God's plan on this earth must be. Help us, O Lord, to an awareness of our spiritual and physical needs, and to help fill the needs of people in all countries of this world—as we give thanks for the food that is set before us. Amen.

$\mathscr{L}$ord, in centuries gone by, the rules were clear and choices were limited. Religious practices were clearly prescribed. People lived their lives in one village. One's station in life and occupation were predetermined. Today, our choices of religious belief and practice, spouse, where to live, what career to follow, and how we conduct our personal lives are almost limitless. Lord, while we cherish these choices and opportunities, help us to choose wisely and in accordance with Thy divine guidance. Amen.

$\mathscr{D}$ear Lord, we thank You for the blessings of friends and family here around Your table. We ask that You make us all truly mindful of Your gifts and help us to share them with others. Amen.

KENT F. WARNER

$\mathcal{L}$ord, we bathe in the soft light of Your eternal love. But we, created in Your image, have assumed the power to destroy humankind, Your creatures, and all that You have created on this holy earth. Help us to insure that the blinding light of a nuclear holocaust shall never occur. Help us, God of love, so that our children and grandchildren, and generations yet to come, may sit at table and praise God as we do now, for the food that they are about to eat. Amen.

$\mathcal{O}$ Lord, how can we thank Thee for the continued mercies received at Thy hands? Each day we have cause to be profoundly grateful unto Thee. Accept our thanks, O Lord, for the great mercies Thou art constantly showing us, and help us to live a good and useful life and to be ever grateful for Thy mercies and love. Amen.

$\mathcal{K}$eep us ever humble, Lord, that we may be the ready recipients of Thy goodness. Deliver us from pride and wickedness, and supply our wants. Amen.

$\mathcal{O}$ dear Heavenly Father, who lookest down upon us in mercy and pitying love, we do thank Thee for our daily repast from Thine earthly store, for our burden is light with Thy grace. Amen.

$\mathcal{H}$ere a little child I stand
Heaving up my either hand;
Cold as paddocks though they be,
Here I lift them up to Thee,
For a benison to fall
On our meat and on us all.

ROBERT HERRICK

53

We thank Thee that here and there are homes made beautiful by Thy presence, lives lived purely and faithfully for Thee, children and child-like souls whose clear and simple trust brings Thee Thyself down amongst men.

J. S. HOWLAND

Give us Lord, a bit o' sun,
A bit o' work and a bit o' fun;
Give us all in the struggle and sputter
Our daily bread and a bit o' butter.

ON THE WALL OF AN OLD INN,
LANCASTER, ENGLAND

Life is good, thank You for this, it could be a lot worse, and I'm grateful it's not. God bless us. More we do not need.

GARRISON KEILLOR

*T*hanks be to Thee, O God, for the order and constancy of nature, summer and winter, seedtime and harvest, and the loveliness of each season in its turn; for a well ordered community, wise government and just laws; for education and the joys of the mind through letters, art and science; for the work we have to do, for strength to do it; for whatever of good there has been in our past lives; and for the hopes and aspirations that lead us on toward better things; for the discipline of life through which we are brought nearer to the common life of men; and for our high calling as servants on earth of Thy Kingdom; we give Thee thanks.

JOHN HUNTER

*A*ll things bright and beautiful.
All creatures great and small,
All things wise and wonderful:
The Lord God made them all.

CECIL FRANCES ALEXANDER

*D*ear Lord we thank You for all the material and spiritual blessings that You shower on us. Help us to share all that we have with those who are less fortunate. Amen.

KENT F. WARNER

*T*hank You for the world so sweet,
Thank You for the food we eat,
Thank You for the birds that sing,
Thank You, God, for everything. Amen.

E. RUTTER LEATHAM

*D*ear Lord, we are all made in Thine image. When we at table "break bread," we may be eating rice, or nan, or pita, or noodles, or matzos, or tortillas, or poi, or white bread. We are all God's race and God's color. Together we are God's family. Amen.